Grammaropolis PRESENTS

WONDERFUL WORDS
FOR FOURTH GRADE

VOCABULARY AND WRITING WORKBOOK

BY ORDER OF

The Mayor of Grammaropolis

Written by Christopher Knight
Interior Design by Christopher Knight
Cover Design by Mckee Frazior
Grammaropolis Character Design by Powerhouse Animation & Mckee Frazior

ISBN: 9781644420546
Copyright © 2021 by Grammaropolis LLC
All rights reserved.
Published by Six Foot Press
Printed in the U.S.A.

Grammaropolis.com
SixFootPress.com

Grammaropolis PRESENTS

WONDERFUL WORDS
FOR FOURTH GRADE

VOCABULARY AND
WRITING WORKBOOK

GRAMMAROPOLIS BOOKS

HOUSTON

FROM THE DESK OF THE MAYOR

Greetings, fellow wordsmith!

Thank you so much for using this workbook. I hope you have fun learning some new vocabulary words!

As you know, many words can act as multiple parts of speech; it all depends on how they're used in the sentence. For the sake of clarity and simplicity (and because we didn't have enough space on the page!), the definitions in this workbook include only one part of speech for each word.

It's great to know a lot of vocabulary words, but the real reason we expand our vocabulary is so that we can communicate more effectively. That's why I've added a writing exercise, with optional prompts, at the end of each section.

Thanks again for visiting Grammaropolis. I hope you enjoy your stay!

—The Mayor

Table of Contents

HOW TO USE THE VOCABULARY PAGES

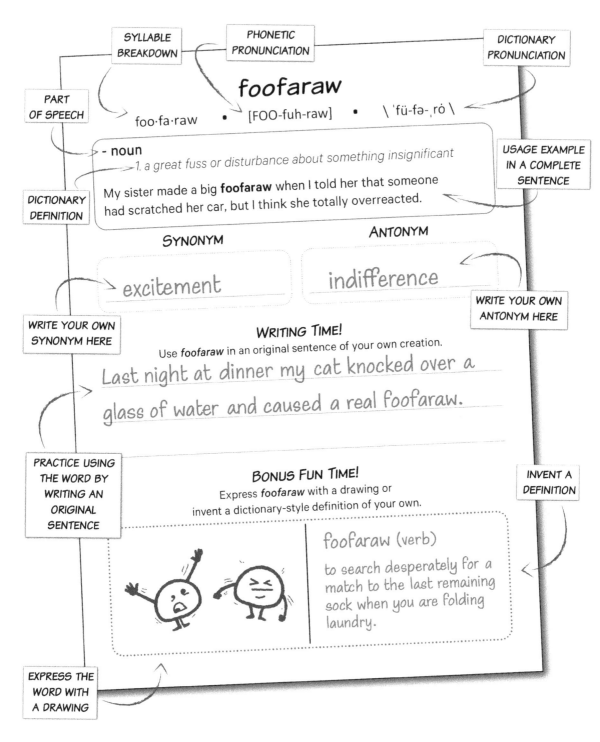

SYLLABLE BREAKDOWN

PHONETIC PRONUNCIATION

DICTIONARY PRONUNCIATION

PART OF SPEECH

foofaraw

foo·fa·raw • [FOO-fuh-raw] • \ ˈfü-fə-ˌrȯ \

- noun
1. a great fuss or disturbance about something insignificant

My sister made a big **foofaraw** when I told her that someone had scratched her car, but I think she totally overreacted.

USAGE EXAMPLE IN A COMPLETE SENTENCE

DICTIONARY DEFINITION

SYNONYM

excitement

ANTONYM

indifference

WRITE YOUR OWN ANTONYM HERE

WRITE YOUR OWN SYNONYM HERE

WRITING TIME!
Use *foofaraw* in an original sentence of your own creation.

Last night at dinner my cat knocked over a glass of water and caused a real foofaraw.

PRACTICE USING THE WORD BY WRITING AN ORIGINAL SENTENCE

BONUS FUN TIME!
Express *foofaraw* with a drawing or invent a dictionary-style definition of your own.

INVENT A DEFINITION

foofaraw (verb)

to search desperately for a match to the last remaining sock when you are folding laundry.

EXPRESS THE WORD WITH A DRAWING

Important Note: Synonyms and antonyms for nouns might be harder to come up with than they are for verbs and adjectives, but do your best!

THE PARTS OF SPEECH REVIEW

Every word acts as at least one of the eight parts of speech. In this workbook, you'll find nouns, verbs, and adjectives. Here are some things you need to remember about them!

NOUNS
A noun can name a person, place, thing, or idea.

Naming a person:
Jason is my very best **friend**.

Naming a place:
Becks Prime is my favorite **restaurant**.

Naming a thing:
That **ball** is my favorite **toy**.

Naming an idea:
Honesty and **loyalty** are my best **qualities**.

VERBS
An action verb expresses mental or physical action, and a linking verb expresses a state of being.

Expressing physical action:
Richard **jumped** across the river.

Expressing mental action:
Richard **considered** jumping across the river.

Expressing a state of being:
Richard **feels** bad. He **is** sorry for jumping across the river.

ADJECTIVES
*An adjective modifies a noun or a pronoun and tells **what kind, which one, how much,** or **how many.***

Modifying a noun:
The **quick brown** fox jumped over the **enormous red** fence at the **first** sign of trouble.

Modifying a pronoun:
They are **satisfied** with the answer, but I am still **curious**.

There are five other parts of speech you won't find in this workbook, but that doesn't mean they're not important!

ADVERBS
*An adverb modifies a verb, an adjective, or another adverb and tells **how, where, when,** or **to what extent.***

PRONOUNS
A pronoun takes the place of one or more nouns or pronouns.

CONJUNCTIONS
A conjunction joins words or word groups.

PREPOSITIONS
A preposition shows a logical relationship or locates an object in time or space.

INTERJECTIONS
An interjection expresses strong or mild emotion.

SECTION ONE: WORD PREVIEW
Welcome to your ten new favorite words!

When you encounter a new word, take a moment to consider what it might mean.

1. Think about the word and circle what part of speech you think it is. *(Many words can act as more than one part of speech, depending on how they're used in the sentence, **so only choose one part of speech below.**)*
2. Come up with a brief definition of the word in the part of speech you've chosen. It doesn't have to be the *correct* definition—just do your best.

demonstrate

Part of Speech: noun verb adjective

*Definition:*_____

_____

carefree

Part of Speech: noun verb adjective

*Definition:*_____

_____

weary

Part of Speech: noun verb adjective

*Definition:*_____

_____

prefer

Part of Speech: noun verb adjective

*Definition:*_____

_____

entire

Part of Speech: noun verb adjective

*Definition:*_____

_____

annual

Part of Speech: noun verb adjective

*Definition:*_____

_____

effective

Part of Speech: noun verb adjective

*Definition:*_____

_____

vacant

Part of Speech: noun verb adjective

*Definition:*_____

_____

threat

Part of Speech: noun verb adjective

*Definition:*_____

_____

extraordinary

Part of Speech: noun verb adjective

*Definition:*_____

_____

demonstrate

dem·on·strate • [dEm-uhn-strayt] • \ ˈdemənˌstrāt \

- verb

1. to give a practical exhibition and explanation of a process;
2. to show the truth with proof or evidence

Kyle **demonstrated** how to log in to his school account.

SYNONYM

ANTONYM

WRITING TIME!

Use *demonstrate* in an original sentence of your own creation.

BONUS FUN TIME!

Express *demonstrate* with a drawing, or
invent a dictionary-style definition of your own.

carefree

care·free   •   [kAIR-free]   •   \ ˈker-ˌfrē \

- adjective
  1. having no worries;
  2. neglectful of consequences

My dad worries all the time, but I am more **carefree**.

SYNONYM

ANTONYM

WRITING TIME!
Use *carefree* in an original sentence of your own creation.

BONUS FUN TIME!
Express *carefree* with a drawing, or
invent a dictionary-style definition of your own.

weary

wea·ry • [wIR-ee] • \ ˈwir-ē \

- adjective
1. *worn out in respect to strength, endurance, or vigor;*
2. *exhausted by suffering or sorrow*

The scout troop was tired and **weary** after the long hike.

SYNONYM

ANTONYM

WRITING TIME!
Use *weary* in an original sentence of your own creation.

BONUS FUN TIME!
Express *weary* with a drawing, or
invent a dictionary-style definition of your own.

prefer

pre·fer   •   [pri-fUHR]   •   \ pri-ˈfər \

- verb

1. to have a preference for : like better

Do you **prefer** milk chocolate or dark chocolate?

SYNONYM

ANTONYM

WRITING TIME!

Use *prefer* in an original sentence of your own creation.

BONUS FUN TIME!

Express *prefer* with a drawing, or
invent a dictionary-style definition of your own.

entire

en·tire   •   [in-tIE-uhr]   •   \ ǝn-ˈtī(ə)r \

- adjective
   1. complete in degree : total;
   2. consisting of one piece

I lost my **entire** progress when my video game crashed!

SYNONYM

ANTONYM

WRITING TIME!
Use *entire* in an original sentence of your own creation.

BONUS FUN TIME!
Express *entire* with a drawing, or
invent a dictionary-style definition of your own.

annual

an·nu·al • [An-yuh-wuhl] • \ ˈan-yə-(wə)l \

- adjective

    1. occurring, appearing, made, done, or acted upon every year or once a year

Every year, we come together for the **annual** pie-throwing contest.

SYNONYM

ANTONYM

WRITING TIME!
Use *annual* in an original sentence of your own creation.

BONUS FUN TIME!
Express *annual* with a drawing, or
invent a dictionary-style definition of your own.

effective

ef·fec·tive • [i-fEk-tiv] • \ əˈfektiv \

> **- adjective**
> 1. *successful in producing a desired or intended result;*
> 2. *capable of being used to a purpose*
>
> Eyeglasses are more **effective** when the lenses are clean.

SYNONYM

ANTONYM

WRITING TIME!
Use *effective* in an original sentence of your own creation.

BONUS FUN TIME!
Express *effective* with a drawing, or
invent a dictionary-style definition of your own.

vacant

va·cant • [vAY-kuhnt] • \ ˈvā-kənt \

- adjective

1. being without content or occupant

The house next door is **vacant** now, but someone will move in soon.

SYNONYM

ANTONYM

WRITING TIME!
Use *vacant* in an original sentence of your own creation.

BONUS FUN TIME!
Express *vacant* with a drawing, or
invent a dictionary-style definition of your own.

threat

threat   •   [thrEt]   •   \ 'thret \

- noun
1. *a person or thing likely to cause damage or danger*
2. *a statement of an intention to inflict hostile action*

This drought is a **threat** to the long-term water supply for all of us.

SYNONYM

ANTONYM

WRITING TIME!
Use *threat* in an original sentence of your own creation.

BONUS FUN TIME!
Express *threat* with a drawing, or
invent a dictionary-style definition of your own.

extraordinary

ex·traor·di·nar·y • [ik-strOR-duh-nair-ee] • \ ikˈstrôrd(ə)nˌerē \

- adjective
1. *very unusual or remarkable;*
2. *unusually great*

Xander's skateboard trick was **extraordinary**; I couldn't believe it!

SYNONYM

ANTONYM

WRITING TIME!
Use *extraordinary* in an original sentence of your own creation.

BONUS FUN TIME!
Express *extraordinary* with a drawing, or
invent a dictionary-style definition of your own.

SECTION ONE: WORD REVIEW

Congratulations on learning ten amazing new words! Remember that the whole point of learning new vocabulary is actually to use it, so let's put your new vocabulary to use.

1. Review the words you've learned. Consider what ideas come to mind when you say the words. How about when you read the definitions?
2. Circle at least **two** of your favorites. You'll get to use these when you write your very own story!

demonstrate —— verb
1. *to give a practical exhibition and explanation of a process;*
2. *to show the truth with proof or evidence*

carefree —— adjective
1. *having no worries;*
2. *neglectful of consequences*

weary —— adjective
1. *worn out in respect to strength, endurance, or vigor;*
2. *exhausted by suffering or sorrow*

prefer —— verb
1. *to have a preference for : like better*

entire —— adjective
1. *complete in degree : total;*
2. *consisting of one piece*

annual —— adjective
1. *occurring, appearing, made, done, or acted upon every year or once a year*

effective —— adjective
1. *successful in producing a desired or intended result;*
2. *capable of being used to a purpose*

vacant —— adjective
1. *being without content or occupant*

threat —— noun
1. *a person or thing likely to cause damage or danger*
2. *a statement of an intention to inflict hostile action*

extraordinary — adjective
1. *very unusual or remarkable;*
2. *unusually great*

STORY ONE

1. List the words you've chosen:

_____

2. Write a story that incorporates all of your chosen words. If you can't think of anything to write about, consider these suggestions:
   - Write a story that takes place inside a video game.
   - Write a story that starts, "This has been the best day of my life."

Title: _____

_____

_____

_____

_____

_____

_____

_____

Wonderful Words for Fourth Grade Vocabulary & Writing Workbook ©2021 Grammaropolis LLC

Caption: _____

Wonderful Words for Fourth Grade Vocabulary & Writing Workbook ©2021 Grammaropolis LLC

SECTION TWO: WORD PREVIEW
Welcome to your ten new favorite words!

When you encounter a new word, take a moment to consider what it might mean.

1. Think about the word and circle what part of speech you think it is. (Many words can act as more than one part of speech, depending on how they're used in the sentence, **so only choose one part of speech below.**)

2. Come up with a brief definition of the word in the part of speech you've chosen. It doesn't have to be the *correct* definition—just do your best.

century
Part of Speech: noun   verb   adjective

Definition:_____

_____

predict
Part of Speech: noun   verb   adjective

Definition:_____

_____

envy
Part of Speech: noun   verb   adjective

Definition:_____

_____

shabby
Part of Speech: noun   verb   adjective

Definition:_____

_____

calculate
Part of Speech: noun   verb   adjective

Definition:_____

_____

noble
Part of Speech: noun   verb   adjective

Definition:_____

_____

distress
Part of Speech: noun   verb   adjective

Definition:_____

_____

select
Part of Speech: noun   verb   adjective

Definition:_____

_____

essential
Part of Speech: noun   verb   adjective

Definition:_____

_____

tidy
Part of Speech: noun   verb   adjective

Definition:_____

_____

century

cen·tu·ry • [sEn-chuhr-ree] • \ ˈsen-ch(ə-)rē \

- noun
   1. a period of 100 years

My 100-year-old granny was born a **century** ago!

SYNONYM

ANTONYM

WRITING TIME!
Use *century* in an original sentence of your own creation.

BONUS FUN TIME!
Express *century* with a drawing, or
invent a dictionary-style definition of your own.

predict

pre·dict   •   [pri-dIkt]   •   \ pri-ˈdikt \

- verb

1. to declare in advance

The weatherman **predicted** rain, and he was actually right this time!

SYNONYM

ANTONYM

WRITING TIME!
Use *predict* in an original sentence of your own creation.

BONUS FUN TIME!
Express *predict* with a drawing, or
invent a dictionary-style definition of your own.

envy

en·vy • [En-vee] • \ ˈenvē \

- verb

1. *to feel envy toward or on account of : be envious of*

I **envy** people who get to eat ice cream for dessert.

SYNONYM

ANTONYM

WRITING TIME!
Use *envy* in an original sentence of your own creation.

BONUS FUN TIME!
Express *envy* with a drawing, or
invent a dictionary-style definition of your own.

shabby

shab·by • [shAb-ee] • \ ˈsha-bē \

- adjective

 1. *threadbare and faded from wear : appearing outworn*

This **shabby** t-shirt may have some holes in it, but I'll wear it anyway.

SYNONYM

ANTONYM

WRITING TIME!
Use *shabby* in an original sentence of your own creation.

BONUS FUN TIME!
Express *shabby* with a drawing, or
invent a dictionary-style definition of your own.

calculate

cal·cu·late • [kAl-kyuh-layt] • \ ˈkal-kyə-ˌlāt \

- verb
1. *to determine by mathematical processes;*
2. *to intend (an action) to have a particular effect*

We just **calculated** that we will run out of food in three days.

SYNONYM

ANTONYM

WRITING TIME!
Use *calculate* in an original sentence of your own creation.

_____

_____

_____

BONUS FUN TIME!
Express *calculate* with a drawing, or
invent a dictionary-style definition of your own.

noble

no·ble   •   [nOH-buhl]   •   \ ˈnō-bəl \

- adjective
    1. possessing outstanding qualities (as of eminence, dignity);
    2. of high birth or exalted rank

I felt so proud and **noble** after helped the kitten down from the tree.

SYNONYM

ANTONYM

WRITING TIME!
Use *noble* in an original sentence of your own creation.

BONUS FUN TIME!
Express *noble* with a drawing, or
invent a dictionary-style definition of your own.

distress

dis·tress   •   [di-strEs]   •   \ dә'stres \

- noun
   1. *extreme anxiety, sorrow, or pain;*
   2. *a state of danger or necessity*

The kitten was meowing in **distress** because it was stuck in a tree.

SYNONYM

ANTONYM

WRITING TIME!
Use *distress* in an original sentence of your own creation.

BONUS FUN TIME!
Express *distress* with a drawing, or
invent a dictionary-style definition of your own.

select

se·lect • [suh-lEkt] • \ sə-ˈlekt \

- verb

1. to choose from a number or group usually by fitness, excellence, or other distinguishing feature

Please **select** your favorite dessert from the menu options.

SYNONYM

ANTONYM

WRITING TIME!
Use *select* in an original sentence of your own creation.

BONUS FUN TIME!
Express *select* with a drawing, or
invent a dictionary-style definition of your own.

essential

es·sen·tial   •   [i-sEn-shuhl]   •   \ i-ˈsen(t)-shəl \

- adjective

1. necessary, indispensable

Learning grammar is an **essential** part of being able to write well.

SYNONYM

ANTONYM

WRITING TIME!
Use *essential* in an original sentence of your own creation.

BONUS FUN TIME!
Express *essential* with a drawing, or
invent a dictionary-style definition of your own.

tidy

ti·dy • [tIE-dee] • \ ˈtī-dē \

- adjective

1. neat and orderly in appearance or habits : kept in good trim : well ordered and cared for

My room is a mess, but my twin sister keeps her room nice and **tidy**.

SYNONYM

ANTONYM

WRITING TIME!
Use *tidy* in an original sentence of your own creation.

BONUS FUN TIME!
Express *tidy* with a drawing, or
invent a dictionary-style definition of your own.

Section Two: Word Review

Congratulations on learning ten amazing new words! Remember that the whole point of learning new vocabulary is actually to use it, so let's put your new vocabulary to use.

1. Review the words you've learned. Consider what ideas come to mind when you say the words. How about when you read the definitions?
2. Circle at least **two** of your favorites. You'll get to use these when you write your very own story!

century ——— noun
1. a period of 100 years

predict ——— verb
1. to declare in advance

envy ——— verb
1. to feel envy toward or on account of : be envious of

shabby ——— adjective
1. threadbare and faded from wear : appearing outworn

calculate ——— verb
1. to determine by mathematical processes;
2. to intend (an action) to have a particular effect

noble ——— adjective
1. possessing outstanding qualities (as of eminence, dignity);
2. of high birth or exalted rank

distress ——— noun
1. extreme anxiety, sorrow, or pain;
2. a state of danger or necessity

select ——— verb
1. to choose from a number or group usually by fitness, excellence, or other distinguishing feature

essential ——— adjective
1. necessary, indispensable

tidy ——— adjective
1. neat and orderly in appearance or habits : kept in good trim : well ordered and cared for

STORY TWO

1. List the words you've chosen:

_____

2. Write a story that incorporates all of your chosen words. If you can't think of anything to write about, consider these suggestions:
   - Write a story that takes place in the year 1600.
   - Write a story that includes a detective and a talking rabbit.

Title: _____

_____

_____

_____

_____

_____

_____

_____

Caption: _____

_____

_____

_____

_____

_____

_____

_____

_____

Wonderful Words for Fourth Grade Vocabulary & Writing Workbook ©2021 Grammaropolis LLC

Welcome to your ten new favorite words!

When you encounter a new word, take a moment to consider what it might mean.

1. Think about the word and circle what part of speech you think it is. *(Many words can act as more than one part of speech, depending on how they're used in the sentence, **so only choose one part of speech below**.)*

2. Come up with a brief definition of the word in the part of speech you've chosen. It doesn't have to be the *correct* definition—just do your best.

accurate
Part of Speech: noun   verb   adjective

Definition:_____

peculiar
Part of Speech: noun   verb   adjective

Definition:_____

flexible
Part of Speech: noun   verb   adjective

Definition:_____

experiment
Part of Speech: noun   verb   adjective

Definition:_____

coax
Part of Speech: noun   verb   adjective

Definition:_____

source
Part of Speech: noun   verb   adjective

Definition:_____

recognize
Part of Speech: noun   verb   adjective

Definition:_____

obvious
Part of Speech: noun   verb   adjective

Definition:_____

congratulate
Part of Speech: noun   verb   adjective

Definition:_____

purpose
Part of Speech: noun   verb   adjective

Definition:_____

accurate

ac·cu·rate   •   [Ak-yuhr-ruht]   •   \ ˈa-kyə-rət \

- adjective
1. free from error or mistake;
2. capable of or successful in reaching the intended target

Please check your answer to make sure that your math is **accurate**.

SYNONYM

ANTONYM

WRITING TIME!
Use *accurate* in an original sentence of your own creation.

BONUS FUN TIME!
Express *accurate* with a drawing, or
invent a dictionary-style definition of your own.

peculiar

pe·cu·liar • [pi-kyOO-lyuhr] • \ pi-ˈkyül-yər \

- adjective
> 1. strange or odd;
> 2. different from the usual or normal

Mr. Cullinan's purple and orange necktie sure is **peculiar**.

SYNONYM

ANTONYM

WRITING TIME!
Use *peculiar* in an original sentence of your own creation.

BONUS FUN TIME!
Express *peculiar* with a drawing, or
invent a dictionary-style definition of your own.

flexible

flex·i·ble   •   [flEk-suh-buhl]   •   \ ˈflek-sə-bəl \

- adjective

1. capable of being turned, bowed, or twisted without breaking;
2. willing or ready to yield to the influence of others

You can't do the pole vault if the pole you're using isn't **flexible**.

SYNONYM

ANTONYM

WRITING TIME!
Use *flexible* in an original sentence of your own creation.

BONUS FUN TIME!
Express *flexible* with a drawing, or
invent a dictionary-style definition of your own.

experiment

ex·per·i·ment • [ik-spAIR-uh-muhnt] • \ ikˈsperəmənt \

> ## - noun
> 1. a course of action tentatively adopted without being sure of the eventual outcome : a test or trial
>
> We conducted an **experiment** to see how much ice cream I could eat.

SYNONYM

ANTONYM

WRITING TIME!
Use *experiment* in an original sentence of your own creation.

BONUS FUN TIME!
Express *experiment* with a drawing, or
invent a dictionary-style definition of your own.

coax

coax • [kOHks] • \ ˈkōkst \

- verb

1. to influence or persuade by gentle urging, caressing, or flattering

Yolanda gently **coaxed** the frightened puppy out from under the bed.

SYNONYM

ANTONYM

WRITING TIME!
Use *coax* in an original sentence of your own creation.

BONUS FUN TIME!
Express *coax* with a drawing, or
invent a dictionary-style definition of your own.

source

source   •   [sORs]   •   \ ˈsȯrs \

- noun
1. *the point of origin;*
2. *a firsthand document or primary reference work*

You have to go to the **source** if you want the cleanest springwater.

SYNONYM

ANTONYM

WRITING TIME!
Use *source* in an original sentence of your own creation.

BONUS FUN TIME!
Express *source* with a drawing, or
invent a dictionary-style definition of your own.

recognize

rec·og·nize • [rEk-ig-niez] • \ ˈre-kig-ˌnīz \

- verb
1. to identify or recall knowledge of something previously known;
2. to acknowledge the existence, validity, or legality of

I **recognize** that girl over there from camp last year.

SYNONYM

ANTONYM

WRITING TIME!
Use *recognize* in an original sentence of your own creation.

BONUS FUN TIME!
Express *recognize* with a drawing, or
invent a dictionary-style definition of your own.

obvious

ob·vi·ous   •   [AHb-vee-uhs]   •   \ ˈäb-vē-əs \

- adjective
>   *1. easily perceived : clear, self-evident, or apparent*

Treating people kindly is an **obvious** way to make good friends.

SYNONYM

ANTONYM

WRITING TIME!
Use *obvious* in an original sentence of your own creation.

BONUS FUN TIME!
Express *obvious* with a drawing, or
invent a dictionary-style definition of your own.

congratulate

con·grat·u·late • [kuhn-grA-chuh-layt] • \ kən-ˈgra-chə-ˌlāt \

- verb

　　1. to express sympathetic pleasure to on account of success or good fortune

Tonya **congratulated** her opponent on a hard-fought victory.

SYNONYM

ANTONYM

WRITING TIME!
Use *congratulate* in an original sentence of your own creation.

_____

_____

_____

BONUS FUN TIME!
Express *congratulate* with a drawing, or
invent a dictionary-style definition of your own.

purpose

pur·pose   •   [pUHR-puhs]   •   \ ˈpər-pəs \

- noun

   1. the reason for which something is done or exists

The **purpose** of learning grammar isn't just to impress your friends.

SYNONYM

ANTONYM

WRITING TIME!
Use *purpose* in an original sentence of your own creation.

BONUS FUN TIME!
Express *purpose* with a drawing, or
invent a dictionary-style definition of your own.

Section Three: Word Review

Congratulations on learning ten amazing new words! Remember that the whole point of learning new vocabulary is actually to use it, so let's put your new vocabulary to use.

1. Review the words you've learned. Consider what ideas come to mind when you say the words. How about when you read the definitions?
2. Circle at least **two** of your favorites. You'll get to use these when you write your very own story!

accurate ———— adjective

1. free from error or mistake;
2. capable of or successful in reaching the intended target

peculiar ———— adjective

1. strange or odd;
2. different from the usual or normal

flexible ———— adjective

1. capable of being turned, bowed, or twisted without breaking;
2. willing or ready to yield to the influence of others

experiment ———— noun

1. a course of action tentatively adopted without being sure of the eventual outcome : a test or trial

coax ———— verb

1. to influence or persuade by gentle urging, caressing, or flattering

source ———— noun

1. the point of origin;
2. a firsthand document or primary reference work

recognize ———— verb

1. to identify or recall knowledge of something previously known;
2. to acknowledge the existence, validity, or legality of

obvious ———— adjective

1. easily perceived : clear, self-evident, or apparent

congratulate ———— verb

1. to express sympathetic pleasure to on account of success or good fortune

purpose ———— noun

1. the reason for which something is done or exists

STORY THREE

1. List the words you've chosen:

_____

2. Write a story that incorporates all of your chosen words. If you can't think of anything to write about, consider these suggestions:
   - **Write a story about the first time you got in trouble.**
   - **Write a story in which the main character can read people's minds.**

Title: _____

_____

_____

_____

_____

_____

_____

_____

Caption: _____

_____

_____

_____

_____

_____

_____

_____

_____

Wonderful Words for Fourth Grade Vocabulary & Writing Workbook ©2021 Grammaropolis LLC

SECTION FOUR: WORD PREVIEW
Welcome to your ten new favorite words!

When you encounter a new word, take a moment to consider what it might mean.

1. Think about the word and circle what part of speech you think it is.
   (Many words can act as more than one part of speech, depending on how they're used in the sentence, **so only choose one part of speech below.**)

2. Come up with a brief definition of the word in the part of speech you've chosen. It doesn't have to be the *correct* definition—just do your best.

summarize
Part of Speech: noun   verb   adjective

*Definition:*_____

_____

tradition
Part of Speech: noun   verb   adjective

*Definition:*_____

_____

portion
Part of Speech: noun   verb   adjective

*Definition:*_____

_____

analyze
Part of Speech: noun   verb   adjective

*Definition:*_____

_____

typical
Part of Speech: noun   verb   adjective

*Definition:*_____

_____

blossom
Part of Speech: noun   verb   adjective

*Definition:*_____

_____

entirety
Part of Speech: noun   verb   adjective

*Definition:*_____

_____

afford
Part of Speech: noun   verb   adjective

*Definition:*_____

_____

simplify
Part of Speech: noun   verb   adjective

*Definition:*_____

_____

response
Part of Speech: noun   verb   adjective

*Definition:*_____

_____

summarize

sum·ma·rize • [sUHm-uhr-riez] • \ ˈsə-mə-ˌrīz \

- verb

1. to tell in or reduce to a summary : present briefly : sum up

I couldn't read the whole book, so will you **summarize** it for me?

SYNONYM

ANTONYM

WRITING TIME!
Use **summarize** in an original sentence of your own creation.

BONUS FUN TIME!
Express **summarize** with a drawing, or
invent a dictionary-style definition of your own.

tradition

tra·di·tion   •   [truh-dIsh-uhn]   •   \ trə-ˈdi-shən \

- noun
1. *a custom or belief passed on from generation to generation;*
2. *a cultural feature preserved or evolved from the past*

Our family's oldest holiday **tradition** is writing letters to one another.

SYNONYM

ANTONYM

WRITING TIME!
Use *tradition* in an original sentence of your own creation.

BONUS FUN TIME!
Express *tradition* with a drawing, or
invent a dictionary-style definition of your own.

portion

por·tion • [pOR-shuhn] • \ ˈpȯr-shən \

- noun

    1. an individual part or share of a whole

You can't have the whole cake, but I'll slice off a nice **portion** for you.

Synonym

Antonym

Writing Time!

Use *portion* in an original sentence of your own creation.

Bonus Fun Time!

Express *portion* with a drawing, or
invent a dictionary-style definition of your own.

analyze

an·a·lyze   •   [An-uh-liez]   •   \ ˈa-nə-ˌlīz \

- verb

   1. to weigh or study (various aspects, factors, or elements) in order to arrive at an answer, result, or solution

Alvin **analyzed** the problem very carefully before making a decision.

SYNONYM

ANTONYM

WRITING TIME!
Use *analyze* in an original sentence of your own creation.

BONUS FUN TIME!
Express *analyze* with a drawing, or
invent a dictionary-style definition of your own.

typical

typ·i·cal   •   [tIp-i-kuhl]   •   \ ˈti-pi-kəl \

- adjective

1. characteristic of a particular person or thing

One of New Mexico's **typical** dishes is called carne adovada.

SYNONYM

ANTONYM

WRITING TIME!

Use *typical* in an original sentence of your own creation.

BONUS FUN TIME!

Express *typical* with a drawing, or
invent a dictionary-style definition of your own.

blossom

blos·som • [blAHs-uhm] • \ ˈblä-səm \

- verb
1. *to mature or develop in a promising or healthy way;*
2. *to unfold like a blossom*

It was amazing to see how much my nephew **blossomed** at camp.

SYNONYM

ANTONYM

WRITING TIME!
Use *blossom* in an original sentence of your own creation.

BONUS FUN TIME!
Express *blossom* with a drawing, or
invent a dictionary-style definition of your own.

entirety

en·tire·ty • [in-tIE-uhr-tee] • \ enˈtī(ə)rtē \

- noun

1. the sum, total, or whole of something

If you can't read the book in its **entirety**, just read the first chapter.

SYNONYM

ANTONYM

WRITING TIME!

Use *entirety* in an original sentence of your own creation.

BONUS FUN TIME!

Express *entirety* with a drawing, or
invent a dictionary-style definition of your own.

afford

af·ford   •   [uh-fORd]   •   \ ə-ˈfȯrd \

> **- verb**
> 1. *to have enough money to pay for;*
> 2. *to be able to do something without serious detriment*
>
> We couldn't **afford** a new car, so we bought a really good used one.

Synonym

Antonym

Writing Time!
Use *afford* in an original sentence of your own creation.

Bonus Fun Time!
Express *afford* with a drawing, or
invent a dictionary-style definition of your own.

simplify

sim·pli·fy • [slm-pluh-fie] • \ ˈsim-plə-ˌfī \

- verb

1. to reduce to basic essentials : divest of superfluous elements

When life gets too complicated, sometimes it helps to **simplify** things.

SYNONYM

ANTONYM

WRITING TIME!
Use *simplify* in an original sentence of your own creation.

BONUS FUN TIME!
Express *simplify* with a drawing, or
invent a dictionary-style definition of your own.

response

re·sponse • [ri-spAHns] • \ ri-ˈspän(t)s \

- **noun**

    1. the act or action of responding (as by an answer);
    2. a responsive or corresponding act or feeling

    The teacher asked a question, but nobody had the correct **response**.

SYNONYM

ANTONYM

WRITING TIME!

Use *response* in an original sentence of your own creation.

BONUS FUN TIME!

Express *response* with a drawing, or
invent a dictionary-style definition of your own.

SECTION FOUR: WORD REVIEW

Congratulations on learning ten amazing new words! Remember that the whole point of learning new vocabulary is actually to use it, so let's put your new vocabulary to use.

1. Review the words you've learned. Consider what ideas come to mind when you say the words. How about when you read the definitions?
2. Circle at least **two** of your favorites. You'll get to use these when you write your very own story!

summarize ——— verb
1. *to tell in or reduce to a summary : present briefly : sum up*

tradition ——— noun
1. *a custom or belief passed on from generation to generation;*
2. *a cultural feature preserved or evolved from the past*

portion ——— noun
1. *an individual part or share of a whole*

analyze ——— verb
1. *to weigh or study (various aspects, factors, or elements) in order to arrive at an answer, result, or solution*

typical ——— adjective
1. *characteristic of a particular person or thing*

blossom ——— verb
1. *to mature or develop in a promising or healthy way;*
2. *to unfold like a blossom*

entirety ——— noun
1. *the sum, total, or whole of something*

afford ——— verb
1. *to have enough money to pay for;*
2. *to be able to do something without serious detriment*

simplify ——— verb
1. *to reduce to basic essentials : divest of superfluous elements*

response ——— noun
1. *the act or action of responding (as by an answer);*
2. *a responsive or corresponding act or feeling*

STORY FOUR

1. List the words you've chosen:

_____

2. Write a story that incorporates all of your chosen words. If you can't think of anything to write about, consider these suggestions:
   - **Write a story that takes place in a laboratory.**
   - **Write a story that starts, "Dear Diary, today I ate a bug."**

Title: _____

_____

_____

_____

_____

_____

_____

_____

Wonderful Words for Fourth Grade Vocabulary & Writing Workbook ©2021 Grammaropolis LLC

Caption: _____

Wonderful Words for Fourth Grade Vocabulary & Writing Workbook ©2021 Grammaropolis LLC

SECTION FIVE: WORD PREVIEW
Welcome to your ten new favorite words!

When you encounter a new word, take a moment to consider what it might mean.

1. Think about the word and circle what part of speech you think it is.
   *(Many words can act as more than one part of speech, depending on how they're used in the sentence, **so only choose one part of speech below**.)*

2. Come up with a brief definition of the word in the part of speech you've chosen. It doesn't have to be the *correct* definition—just do your best.

contrast
Part of Speech: noun   verb   adjective

*Definition:*_____

_____

valiant
Part of Speech: noun   verb   adjective

*Definition:*_____

_____

frontier
Part of Speech: noun   verb   adjective

*Definition:*_____

_____

surface
Part of Speech: noun   verb   adjective

*Definition:*_____

_____

ancestor
Part of Speech: noun   verb   adjective

*Definition:*_____

_____

fortunate
Part of Speech: noun   verb   adjective

*Definition:*_____

_____

inspire
Part of Speech: noun   verb   adjective

*Definition:*_____

_____

accomplish
Part of Speech: noun   verb   adjective

*Definition:*_____

_____

represent
Part of Speech: noun   verb   adjective

*Definition:*_____

_____

jagged
Part of Speech: noun   verb   adjective

*Definition:*_____

_____

contrast

con·trast   •   [kuhn-trAst]   •   \ ˈkän-ˌtrast \

- noun

1. the divergence between objects in juxtaposition or close association

The **contrast** between the two tennis players' styles was enormous.

SYNONYM

ANTONYM

WRITING TIME!
Use *contrast* in an original sentence of your own creation.

BONUS FUN TIME!
Express *contrast* with a drawing, or
invent a dictionary-style definition of your own.

valiant

tra·di·tion   •   [vAl-yuhnt]   •   \ ˈval-yənt \

> **- adjective**
>   *1. possessing or acting with bravery or boldness*
>
> A good knight is both **valiant** and kind.

Synonym

Antonym

Writing Time!
Use *valiant* in an original sentence of your own creation.

Bonus Fun Time!
Express *valiant* with a drawing, or
invent a dictionary-style definition of your own.

frontier

fron·tier • [fruhn-tIR] • \ ˌfrənˈtir \

- noun

1. a zone or region that forms the margin of settled or developed territory

We rode our bikes all the way out to the neighborhood's **frontier**.

SYNONYM

ANTONYM

WRITING TIME!
Use *frontier* in an original sentence of your own creation.

BONUS FUN TIME!
Express *frontier* with a drawing, or
invent a dictionary-style definition of your own.

surface

sur·face • [sUHR-fuhs] • \ ˈsər-fəs \

- noun

1. the exterior or outside of an object or body : one or more of the faces of a three-dimensional thing

You'll have to polish the **surface** of my car with a soft cloth.

SYNONYM

ANTONYM

WRITING TIME!

Use *surface* in an original sentence of your own creation.

BONUS FUN TIME!

Express *surface* with a drawing, or
invent a dictionary-style definition of your own.

ancestor

an·ces·tor • [An-ses-tuhr] • \ ˈan-ˌse-stər \

- noun
1. *one from whom a person is descended, typically more remote than a grandparent*

My **ancestors** came to this country over a hundred years ago.

SYNONYM

ANTONYM

WRITING TIME!
Use *ancestor* in an original sentence of your own creation.

BONUS FUN TIME!
Express *ancestor* with a drawing, or
invent a dictionary-style definition of your own.

fortunate

for·tu·nate • [fOR-chuh-nuht] • \ ˈfȯrch-nət \

- **adjective**

1. coming by good luck or favorable chance;
2. receiving some unforeseen or unexpected good

Frank knew he was **fortunate** that the referee didn't call a foul.

SYNONYM

ANTONYM

WRITING TIME!
Use *fortunate* in an original sentence of your own creation.

BONUS FUN TIME!
Express *fortunate* with a drawing, or
invent a dictionary-style definition of your own.

inspire

in·spire   •   [in-splE-uhr]   •   \ ə̇nzˈpī(ə)r \

- verb

1. to influence, move, or guide (as to speech or action)

Mrs. Urrea **inspired** the class with stories of her volunteer work.

SYNONYM

ANTONYM

WRITING TIME!

Use *inspire* in an original sentence of your own creation.

BONUS FUN TIME!

Express *inspire* with a drawing, or
invent a dictionary-style definition of your own.

accomplish

ac·com·plish • [uh-kAHm-plish] • \ə-ˈkäm-plish \

- **verb**

    1. to achieve or complete successfully : execute fully

If you really set your mind to it, you can **accomplish** anything.

SYNONYM

ANTONYM

WRITING TIME!
Use *accomplish* in an original sentence of your own creation.

BONUS FUN TIME!
Express *accomplish* with a drawing, or
invent a dictionary-style definition of your own.

represent

rep·re·sent • [rep-ri-zEnt] • \ ˌreprəˈzent \

- verb

1. to serve as a sign or symbol of

The stars on the United States flag **represent** the fifty states.

SYNONYM

ANTONYM

WRITING TIME!

Use *represent* in an original sentence of your own creation.

BONUS FUN TIME!

Express *represent* with a drawing, or
invent a dictionary-style definition of your own.

jagged

jag·ged   •   [jAgUHd]   •   \ ˈja-gəd \

- **adjective**
  1. having a sharply uneven edge or surface

  I sliced my finger on a **jagged** rock down by the stream.

SYNONYM

ANTONYM

WRITING TIME!
Use *jagged* in an original sentence of your own creation.

BONUS FUN TIME!
Express *jagged* with a drawing, or
invent a dictionary-style definition of your own.

SECTION FIVE: WORD REVIEW

Congratulations on learning ten amazing new words! Remember that the whole point of learning new vocabulary is actually to use it, so let's put your new vocabulary to use.

1. Review the words you've learned. Consider what ideas come to mind when you say the words. How about when you read the definitions?
2. Circle at least **two** of your favorites. You'll get to use these when you write your very own story!

contrast ——————— noun

1. the divergence between objects in juxtaposition or close association

valiant ——————— adjective

1. possessing or acting with bravery or boldness

frontier ——————— noun

1. a zone or region that forms the margin of settled or developed territory

surface ——————— noun

1. the exterior or outside of an object or body : one or more of the faces of a three-dimensional thing

ancestor ——————— noun

1. one from whom a person is descended, typically more remote than a grandparent

fortunate ——————— adjective

1. coming by good luck or favorable chance;
2. receiving some unforeseen or unexpected good

inspire ——————— verb

1. to influence, move, or guide (as to speech or action)

accomplish ——————— verb

1. to achieve or complete successfully : execute fully

represent ——————— verb

1. to serve as a sign or symbol of

jagged ——————— adjective

1. having a sharply uneven edge or surface

STORY FIVE

1. List the words you've chosen:

2. Write a story that incorporates all of your chosen words. If you can't think of anything to write about, consider these suggestions:
   - **Write a story that starts with you ordering a pizza.**
   - **Write a story that takes place inside a big structure at the bottom of the ocean.**

Title: _____

Caption: _____

SECTION SIX: WORD PREVIEW
Welcome to your ten new favorite words!

When you encounter a new word, take a moment to consider what it might mean.

1. Think about the word and circle what part of speech you think it is.
   (*Many words can act as more than one part of speech, depending on how they're used in the sentence, **so only choose one part of speech below**.*)

2. Come up with a brief definition of the word in the part of speech you've chosen. It doesn't have to be the *correct* definition—just do your best.

crafty
Part of Speech: noun   verb   adjective

Definition:_____

impact
Part of Speech: noun   verb   adjective

Definition:_____

temporary
Part of Speech: noun   verb   adjective

Definition:_____

develop
Part of Speech: noun   verb   adjective

Definition:_____

eager
Part of Speech: noun   verb   adjective

Definition:_____

maximum
Part of Speech: noun   verb   adjective

Definition:_____

complete
Part of Speech: noun   verb   adjective

Definition:_____

indicate
Part of Speech: noun   verb   adjective

Definition:_____

communicate
Part of Speech: noun   verb   adjective

Definition:_____

awkward
Part of Speech: noun   verb   adjective

Definition:_____

crafty

craft·y   •   [krAf-tee]   •   \ ˈkraf-tē \

- adjective
1. skillful, clever, ingenious

Only a **crafty** person would figure out how to hang those patio lights.

SYNONYM

ANTONYM

WRITING TIME!
Use *crafty* in an original sentence of your own creation.

BONUS FUN TIME!
Express *crafty* with a drawing, or
invent a dictionary-style definition of your own.

impact

im·pact • [Im-pakt] • \ impakt \

- noun
  1. *the force of impression of one thing on another*

The **impact** of an asteroid hitting the earth would be catastrophic.

SYNONYM

ANTONYM

WRITING TIME!
Use *impact* in an original sentence of your own creation.

BONUS FUN TIME!
Express *impact* with a drawing, or
invent a dictionary-style definition of your own.

temporary

tem·po·rary • [tEm-puhr-rair-ee] • \ ˈtem-pə-ˌrer-ē \

- adjective

1. lasting for a time only : existing or continuing for a limited time

You don't have to live there forever; it's only a **temporary** solution.

SYNONYM

ANTONYM

WRITING TIME!
Use *temporary* in an original sentence of your own creation.

BONUS FUN TIME!
Express *temporary* with a drawing, or
invent a dictionary-style definition of your own.

develop

de·vel·op • [di-vEl-uhp] • \ dəˈveləp \

- verb

1. *to grow or cause to grow and become more mature, advanced, or elaborate*

As my survival skills **developed**, I became more comfortable outside.

SYNONYM

ANTONYM

WRITING TIME!

Use *develop* in an original sentence of your own creation.

BONUS FUN TIME!

Express *develop* with a drawing, or
invent a dictionary-style definition of your own.

eager

ea·ger • [EEgUHR] • \ ˈēgər \

- adjective
  1. *characterized by strong and urgent interest, desire, ardor, enthusiasm, or impatience*

  We were all **eager** to finish class so that we could go out and play.

SYNONYM

ANTONYM

WRITING TIME!
Use *eager* in an original sentence of your own creation.

BONUS FUN TIME!
Express *eager* with a drawing, or
invent a dictionary-style definition of your own.

maximum

max·i·mum   •   [mAk-suh-muhm]   •   \ ˈmaksəməm \

- adjective
    1. greatest in quantity or highest in degree attainable or attained

If you want to climb that mountain, you must give **maximum** effort.

SYNONYM

ANTONYM

WRITING TIME!
Use *maximum* in an original sentence of your own creation.

BONUS FUN TIME!
Express *maximum* with a drawing, or
invent a dictionary-style definition of your own.

complete

com·plete   •   [kuhm-plEEt]   •   \ kəm-ˈplēt \

- adjective

1. possessing all necessary parts, items, components, or elements

Is this the **complete** menu, or is it just part of what you offer?

SYNONYM

ANTONYM

WRITING TIME!
Use *complete* in an original sentence of your own creation.

BONUS FUN TIME!
Express *complete* with a drawing, or
invent a dictionary-style definition of your own.

indicate

in·di·cate • [In-duh-kayt] • \ ˈində͟ˌkāt \

> **- verb**
>   1. *to point out;*
>   2. *to show the probable existence of : give fair evidence of*
>
> Please **indicate** the correct answer by tapping it with your finger.

SYNONYM

ANTONYM

WRITING TIME!
Use *indicate* in an original sentence of your own creation.

BONUS FUN TIME!
Express *indicate* with a drawing, or
invent a dictionary-style definition of your own.

communicate

com·mu·ni·cate • [kuh-myOO-nuh-kayt] • \ kə-ˈmyü-nə-ˌkāt \

- verb

1. *to make known : convey the knowledge or information of*

Let's **communicate** our wishes beforehand so we get what we want.

SYNONYM

ANTONYM

WRITING TIME!
Use *communicate* in an original sentence of your own creation.

BONUS FUN TIME!
Express *communicate* with a drawing, or
invent a dictionary-style definition of your own.

awkward

awk·ward   •   [AWk-wuhrd]   •   \ ˈȯ-kwərd \

- **adjective**
    1. lacking social grace and assurance;
    2. feeling or showing embarrassment : ill at ease

I feel so **awkward** whenever I get out on the dance floor.

SYNONYM

ANTONYM

WRITING TIME!
Use *awkward* in an original sentence of your own creation.

BONUS FUN TIME!
Express *awkward* with a drawing, or
invent a dictionary-style definition of your own.

SECTION SIX: WORD REVIEW

Congratulations on learning ten amazing new words! Remember that the whole point of learning new vocabulary is actually to use it, so let's put your new vocabulary to use.

1. Review the words you've learned. Consider what ideas come to mind when you say the words. How about when you read the definitions?
2. Circle at least **two** of your favorites. You'll get to use these when you write your very own story!

crafty —— adjective
1. skillful, clever, ingenious

impact —— noun
1. the force of impression of one thing on another

temporary —— adjective
1. lasting for a time only : existing or continuing for a limited time

develop —— verb
1. to grow or cause to grow and become more mature, advanced, or elaborate

eager —— adjective
1. characterized by strong and urgent interest, desire, ardor, enthusiasm, or impatience

maximum —— adjective
1. greatest in quantity or highest in degree attainable or attained

complete —— adjective
1. possessing all necessary parts, items, components, or elements

indicate —— verb
1. to point out;
2. to show the probable existence of : give fair evidence of

communicate —— verb
1. to make known : convey the knowledge or information of

awkward —— adjective
1. lacking social grace and assurance;
2. feeling or showing embarrassment : ill at ease

STORY SIX

1. List the words you've chosen:

_____

2. Write a story that incorporates all of your chosen words. If you can't think of anything to write about, consider these suggestions:

   - **Write a story in which you have to eat all of your meals (even breakfast and dinner) in the school cafeteria every day.**

   - **Write a story about you getting to meet your number one hero.**

Title: _____

_____

_____

_____

_____

_____

_____

_____

Wonderful Words for Fourth Grade Vocabulary & Writing Workbook ©2021 Grammaropolis LLC

Caption: _____

INDEX OF WORDS USED

CPSIA information can be obtained
at www.ICGtesting.com
Printed in the USA
JSHW020743290821
18255JS00002B/3

9 781644 420546